W9-BCI-666

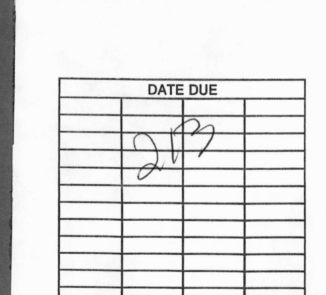

DATE DUE

ABOVE &
BEYOND

ASTRONAUTS

Published by Smart Apple Media

123 South Broad Street

Mankato, Minnesota 56001

Copyright © 2000 Smart Apple Media.

International copyright reserved in all countries. No part

of this book may be reproduced in any form without written

permission from the publisher.

Printed in the United States of America.

Photos: nasa/kennedy space center/johnson space center;

page 7–corbis/marc garanger; page 8–corbis/bettmann

Design and Production: EvansDay Design

Library of Congress Cataloging-in-Publication Data

Richardson, Adele, 1966–

Astronauts / by Adele D. Richardson

p. cm. — (Above and beyond)

Includes index.

Summary: Examines the history and missions of manned space

flight and the training and duties of both American

and Russian astronauts.

ISBN 1-58340-046-X

1. Astronautics—Juvenile literature. 2. Astronauts—Juvenile

literature. [1. Astronauts. 2. Manned space flight.] I. Title.

II. Series: Above and beyond (Mankato, Minn.)

TL793.R528   1999

629.45'0092'2—DC21   98-41865

3 5 7 9 8 6 4 2

ASTRONAUTS

ADELE D. RICHARDSON

ABOVE &
BEYOND

ROCKET ENGINES ROARED to life with a burst of blinding light ✳ The ground trembled for miles around the Kennedy Space Center as the shuttle lifted gracefully off the launch pad ✳ Inside, the astronauts, strapped into their seats, held on tightly as the shuttle shook violently beneath them ✳ Minutes later, the spacecraft calmed down and was soon speeding smoothly toward space ✳ Looking out the shuttle's front windows, the astronauts watched the blue sky darken to an inky blackness dotted with twinkling stars ✳ They had made it into space ✳

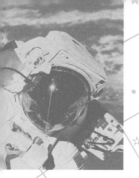

Pioneers
of Space

On October 4, 1957, the Soviet Union surprised the world by launching *Sputnik 1*, the first **satellite**, into orbit. One month later, *Sputnik 2* was launched with a dog named Laika, the first living creature to enter space, on board. The Russians had taken the first steps in space exploration.

The United States, not wanting to be left behind, launched its first satellite, *Explorer 1*, on January 31, 1958. More powerful rockets were soon designed and built. Americans hoped to catch up to the Soviets by being the first nation to launch a man into space. On October 1, 1958, the National Aeronautics and Space Administration (NASA) was created to oversee the country's new space program. Just months later, in March 1959, NASA leapt forward when its *Pioneer 4* spacecraft became the first space exploration vehicle to reach the moon.

The first living creature to test space flight for the U.S. was a monkey named Ham. On January 12, 1961, the monkey was launched in a capsule that was airborne for nearly 17 minutes before splashing into the Atlantic Ocean. Soon an American **astronaut** would experience the same flight. But the Russians were again one step ahead. On April 12, 1961, **cosmonaut** Yuri Gagarin became the first human in space when he circled the earth for 108 minutes aboard *Vostok 1*.

A **satellite** is an object—natural or man-made—that orbits a celestial body.

An **astronaut** is a person who travels above the earth's atmosphere.

Cosmonaut is the name given to astronauts from the Soviet Union.

The earliest American manned space flight program was called Project Mercury. The project had three main goals: to orbit the earth with a manned spacecraft; to discover if humans could function well in space; and to safely return both man and spacecraft to Earth.

There were eight manned flights for this project. Each

Laika the dog, represented in a Sputnik 2 replica here, became the first living creature to travel through space.

would carry one passenger (two of the flights used monkeys). The first human passenger, a military aircraft pilot named Alan Shepard, finally experienced space flight on May 5, 1961. Although Shepard's flight lasted only about 15 minutes, it offered hope for the rest of the program. On May 25, 1961, President John F. Kennedy challenged NASA to land an American on the moon before the end of the decade.

As NASA developed the spacecraft that would carry men to the moon, the Mercury astronauts continued with the program. Virgil (Gus) Grissom was the next man into space; his mission would be a repeat of Shepard's. Grissom's spacecraft, *Liberty Bell 7*, was launched

Cosmonaut Yuri Gagarin—the first man to orbit the earth.

on July 21, 1961, and stayed in flight for 15 minutes and 37 seconds. When Grissom splashed down in the ocean, however, a problem with the side hatch caused the spacecraft to sink, nearly drowning the astronaut.

After a monkey named Enos was used to further test space flight in November 1961, astronaut John Glenn made history. On February 20, 1962, the future senator from Ohio became the first American to completely circle Earth, which he did three times. Three more flights followed Glenn's before Project Mercury ended in 1963. The longest flight was that of L. Gordon Cooper on May 15, 1963. Cooper, who is the only astronaut to claim to have seen a UFO (Unidentified Flying Object), remained in orbit for 34 hours and 19 seconds, proving that man could indeed function in space.

The seven Mercury astronauts became American heroes.

Project Gemini

As Project Mercury came to a close, both the Soviet Union and the U.S. seemed to set new space records with every launch. America's next program, Project Gemini, would be no exception.

Project Gemini, which lasted slightly more than one and a half years, involved 10 manned space flights and several unmanned rocket testings. For the first time, space flights could have two astronauts on board instead of just one. The goals for this project included determining whether humans could survive safely in space for long periods of time; practicing **docking** while in orbit; and seeing if humans could function outside of a spacecraft. Astronauts would need to be able to do all of these things before a landing on the moon would be possible.

One of the most impressive events during Project Gemini happened on June 3, 1965, when astronaut Edward White II became the first American to engage in **extravehicular activity (EVA)**, more commonly called a "space walk." White spent 21 minutes outside of his spacecraft, using a hand-held maneuvering unit astronauts called "the gun" to move around. For safety, he was attached to

Walking in space is a thrilling yet dangerous part of an astronaut's work.

the spacecraft with a 24-foot (7 m) line to keep from float-ing away into space.

Gemini astronauts also practiced docking with un-manned spacecraft launched from the Kennedy Space Center in Florida. Being able to dock precisely would be a critical skill during a moon landing. While part of the spacecraft would remain in orbit, another section called

Docking *is the physical connection of two spacecraft in space.*

An **extravehicular activity** *(EVA) is any activity performed in space outside a spacecraft.*

the **lunar lander** would detach and land on the moon's surface. Once the moon exploration was over, the lander would have to lift off from the surface and dock with the orbiting spacecraft before the astronauts could return home.

The last launch for Gemini took place on November 11, 1966. By the end of the project, astronauts had spent thousands of hours in space preparing for a future moon mission. More than 12 of those hours had been spent on space

*A **lunar lander** is a part of an orbiting spacecraft that can detach and land on the moon.*

Astronaut Scott Carpenter during training at the Johnson Space Center.

walks. The astronauts had also conducted many scientific experiments and studies of Earth while in orbit.

The American public felt ready for the country to take the next great step: a manned landing on the moon. The biggest concern was whether the Soviet Union would again beat the U.S. to it. While the Gemini astronauts had been training, the Soviet Union's cosmonauts had also been launching manned spacecraft, docking, and walking in space.

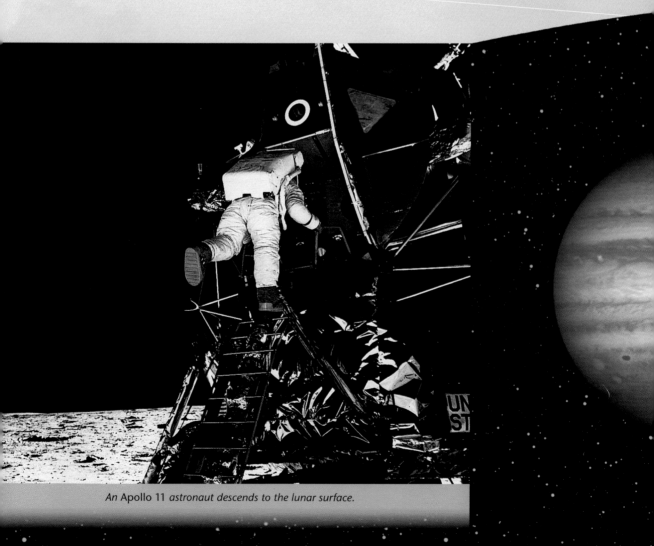

An Apollo 11 *astronaut descends to the lunar surface.*

One Giant Leap

Project Apollo, the program that would take American astronauts to the moon, did not get off to a good start. On January 27, 1967, three astronauts—Gus Grissom, Edward White II, and Roger Chaffee—were testing *Apollo 1*'s equipment while the spacecraft sat on the launch pad. At 6:31 PM Eastern Time, a fire started inside the spacecraft. It spread so quickly that none of the astronauts had a chance to escape—all three were killed.

The deaths were the first in NASA history, and the manned space program was put on hold while officials investigated the cause of the fire. The program did not continue until *Apollo 7* was launched on October 11, 1968.

The most historic launch of Project Apollo took place on July 16, 1969. On board *Apollo 11* were Neil Armstrong, Michael Collins, and Edwin "Buzz" Aldrin. Four days after lifting off from the Kennedy Space Center, the lunar lander touched down on the surface of the moon. At 10:59 PM Eastern Time, Armstrong accomplished the goal set by President Kennedy more than eight years earlier. He stepped on the moon and spoke the famous words: "That's one small step for man, one giant leap for mankind." The accomplishment was especially fulfilling for Armstrong, who had earned his pilot's license by the age of 16 and had devoted his life to flying.

Apollo 11 remained on the moon for only a few hours. The astronauts stayed long enough to collect some samples to bring back to Earth and to leave an American flag at the landing site. Also left behind was a plaque stating: HERE MEN FROM THE PLANET EARTH FIRST SET FOOT UPON THE MOON JULY 1969 A.D. WE CAME IN PEACE FOR ALL

This Apollo 17 astronaut was one of the last Americans on the moon.

MANKIND. The three astronauts landed safely back on Earth on July 24, 1969. The U.S. had finally moved ahead of the Soviet Union in the **space race**.

Apollo 12's mission, launched on November 14, 1969, was a nearly perfect trip to the moon and back. After this mission, the American public seemed to lose interest in the space program. That would change, however, after Apollo 13 was launched on April 11, 1970.

An exploding oxygen tank in the **service module** crippled Apollo 13, forcing its three-man crew to move to the

*The **service module** is the part of a spacecraft that stores electrical power and oxygen.*

*The **space race**—between Americans and Russians—was a race for space supremacy.*

One of the first footprints left on the moon by Apollo 11 astronauts.

lunar lander while it traveled to the moon. The plan was to use the moon's gravity to turn the spacecraft around. As the astronauts shut down the electrical systems to save power, the temperature in the lander dropped to 38 degrees Fahrenheit (3 degrees C). To breathe, the crew had to raid oxygen stored in the spacesuits. It was only through the hard work and determination of the astronauts and the NASA crews on the ground that *Apollo 13* was brought safely back to Earth.

In all, 12 American astronauts—over the course of six missions—set foot on the moon. Alan Shepard, the first American into space, made his visit to the moon a historic

Astronaut Jim Lowell during the ill-fated Apollo 13 *mission.*

one by hitting golf balls around the lunar surface. *Apollo 17*, the last mission to the moon, was launched on December 7, 1972. Before the astronauts left the lunar surface, a second plaque was placed near the landing site. It read: HERE MAN COMPLETED HIS FIRST EXPLORATIONS OF THE MOON DECEMBER 1972 A.D. MAY THE SPIRIT OF PEACE IN WHICH WE CAME BE REFLECTED IN THE LIVES OF ALL MANKIND. No humans have returned to the moon since.

The flight of NASA's first space shuttle in 1981 marked the beginning of a new era in space exploration. As America's space program continued to enjoy success, no one could have foretold that the worst disaster in space exploration history was about to happen.

On the cold morning of January 28, 1986, the space shuttle *Challenger* rose from the launch pad. Seventy-three seconds into flight, a part on one of the rocket boosters failed, causing the shuttle to explode in a giant ball of fire. All seven astronauts on board were killed, including Christa McAuliffe, an elementary school teacher. More than two years would pass before another shuttle was launched.

The tragic loss of life in the Challenger explosion stunned the world.

The
Right Stuff

The first seven Mercury astronauts were chosen from more than 100 candidates. Since no one knew exactly what to expect from space travel, the requirements to become an astronaut were very strict. To be one of the first astronauts, a person had to be 30 to 40 years of age and shorter than 5 feet, 11 inches (1.8 m) tall. Astronauts also needed to be test pilots for the military and to have already piloted 1,500 hours in a jet. In addition to having an engineering degree, space travelers had to be in excellent physical and mental condition and be able to stay calm under pressure.

Today, rockets are no longer used for manned space flights; instead, astronauts are carried from Earth by space shuttles. With the invention of the space shuttle came a change in NASA's admission policies. On August 1, 1985, the space agency began continuously accepting astronaut applications.

To become a member of the U.S. astronaut corps today, an applicant must be a U.S. citizen, be in good physical and mental condition, and hold at least a bachelor's degree in mathematics, engineering, or physical science.

Astronaut John Glenn prepares to make history in 1962.

Having the right stuff also depends on which type of astronaut a person wants to be.

Pilot astronaut applicants must be between 5 feet, 4 inches (1.6 m) and 6 feet, 4 inches (2 m) tall, and have at least 1,000 hours of jet aircraft flying experience. A **mission specialist** is an astronaut trained to conduct scien-

A **pilot astronaut** *is an astronaut who flies the shuttle.*

A **mission specialist** *is an astronaut trained to conduct scientific experiments.*

tific experiments. These astronauts don't need to have any piloting experience, but they must have at least three years of professional experience related to their mission. Mission specialists must all be between 5 feet (1.5 m) and 6 feet, 4 inches (2 m) tall.

A third type of astronaut is a **payload specialist**, who usually works for the owner of the payload, or cargo, being carried into space. Payload specialists usually are not career astronauts; sometimes they don't even work for NASA. But even privately hired astronauts must go through basic training before they can fly.

Although a person must be an American citizen to join

*A **payload specialist** is an astronaut who handles the cargo on a specific mission.*

At the age of 77, John Glenn (left) returned to space in October 1998.

the astronaut corps, people of other nationalities can ride in the space shuttle as long as NASA approves their qualifications before launch. Since 1969, more than 200 astronauts worldwide have been flown into orbit.

Only the most qualified applicants are chosen by NASA to become astronaut candidates. Those chosen then go through a series of mental and physical tests to see if they can handle the stress of a dangerous job. The final test is an interview by several active astronauts to determine if the applicant would be a good crew mate. Once selected, candidates who want to become a pilot or mission specialist go through one year of training at the Johnson Space Center in Houston, Texas, before they are officially called astronauts.

American and Canadian astronauts sometimes work together on missions in space.

Astronauts in training spend a lot of time in the class-room, studying everything imaginable concerning space flight and spacecraft construction. Flight training is another part of being an astronaut candidate. Both shuttle pilot and mission specialist hopefuls are taken up in a jet aircraft, where they practice maneuvering and study the jet's life support and electrical systems.

To experience weightlessness, the astronaut candidates are taken for a ride in a large airplane with heavily padded inside walls. The plane goes through a series of climbs and dives while flying at a high altitude. As it reaches the top part of its climb and begins to head downward, passengers experience what it feels like to float in space. An unfortunate side effect of weightlessness is nausea, which is why NASA has nicknamed the plane "The Vomit Comet."

To keep from feeling sick while in orbit, some astronauts place medicated pads behind their ears. The pads are soaked in a medicine that prevents nausea. As the pads are worn, the medicine is slowly absorbed into the astronauts' skin, going to work inside their bodies.

Survival training is another essential part of an astronaut's preparation. If a shuttle is forced to land in the sea or a remote area, its astronauts need to know how to take

Astronauts in training are first introduced to weightlessness in NASA's "Vomit Comet."

care of themselves. They are taught to use parachutes and how to survive in water until help arrives.

Astronaut candidates also learn to become comfortable with space equipment such as the **manned maneuvering unit (MMU)**, a backpack-shaped power device used to move around during space walks. Sometimes they spend time operating equipment underwater to simulate the feeling of wearing bulky spacesuits.

After the year-long basic training is complete, the graduates join the astronaut corps and continue to train until they are assigned a mission. Then they will move to advanced or flight specific training.

During advanced training, the astronauts practice using every piece of equipment on the shuttle. Tests are run continuously to familiarize the astronauts with flying, landing, and using the remote-controlled arm in the cargo bay. One of the most useful tools in advanced training is the **Shuttle Mission Simulator (SMS)**. This machine, which is an exact copy of the shuttle's instrument panels, can help the crew practice every aspect of a mission from launch to landing.

*The **Shuttle Mission Simulator** (SMS) is a computerized instrument used in astronaut training.*

*The **manned maneuvering unit** (MMU) is a device used during space walks.*

Flight specific training helps the crew train for tasks they must perform during a particular flight. The crew begins practicing on the SMS about 11 weeks before the actual mission. The purpose of the mission could be anything from launching a new satellite into orbit to fixing or retrieving an older one.

Astronauts practice basic and advanced training every day until they are chosen for a mission. After the mission is confirmed, other astronauts spend less time practicing so that the shuttle crew can spend as much time as possible on the simulators.

Astronauts spend time training underwater (left); Dr. Roberta Bondar (right), the first Canadian woman to fly in space.

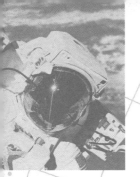

An Astronaut's Life

Life is very different for astronauts in space than it is on the ground. One of the most amazing effects of space travel is that people tend to "grow" one or two inches (2.5 to 5 cm) in a weightless environment. This happens because the vertebrae in a person's spine are no longer held tightly together by gravity. Once they land on Earth, however, astronauts return to their normal height.

Because their bones don't have to support their body weight, astronauts lose calcium. With no gravity to resist movement, muscles can also become very weak. If an astronaut is spending a lot of time in orbit, he or she must use exercise equipment—such as rowing machines, exercise bikes, and treadmills—to keep fit.

Astronauts never walk while in **zero gravity**. Instead, they float or glide from place to place. This, like everything else, takes some practice, and the astronauts must be careful not to smash into anything important.

Bathing is also a unique experience in space. Astronauts in orbit cannot take a bath or shower like they can on Earth, because the water droplets would float all over the shuttle and damage its sophisticated equipment. To keep clean, astronauts simply wipe themselves with specially treated washcloths.

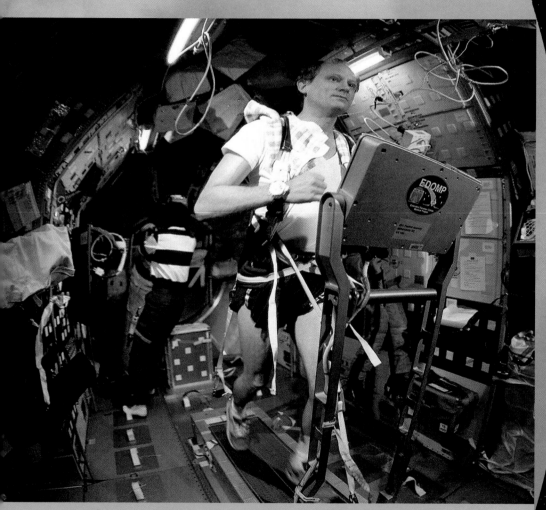

Astronauts in space for long periods of time must exercise to stay strong.

Zero gravity *is a term astronauts use for weightlessness in Earth's orbit.*

MARCH 22, 1995

Cosmonaut Valery Polyakov completes a record 438 days in space aboard Mir.

Most everyday things such as eating and sleeping take some getting used to in a weightless environment. At mealtimes, many astronauts float around the shuttle as they eat, being careful not to crash into anyone or to let their food get away from them.

Sleeping also presents an interesting challenge. It would do no good to have regular beds in the shuttle, since the astronauts would just float off of them. To sleep,

Working in a shuttle's cargo bay is a common astronaut duty.

many astronauts strap themselves into a special sleeping bag that's slightly inflated to make it feel like a mattress on Earth. Others may tie themselves to a part of the shuttle and take a quick nap.

Missions in space may include a space walk to fix a damaged satellite or to place a new one into orbit. Many times the **Remote Manipulator System (RMS)** is used for these jobs. This long arm can easily pluck a satellite from orbit and place it in the shuttle's cargo bay. The astronauts' other activities often involve conducting experiments with medicine, plants, or animals.

Astronauts train continuously for years to master the skills needed to live and work in space. For nearly 40 years, NASA has sent these courageous pioneers into space to do dangerous jobs for the benefit of the U.S. and all of mankind. No one knows what the future of space exploration holds, but we can be sure that astronauts will continue to lead the way.

*The **Remote Manipulator System** (RMS) is a 50-foot (16 m) remote-controlled arm on a shuttle.*

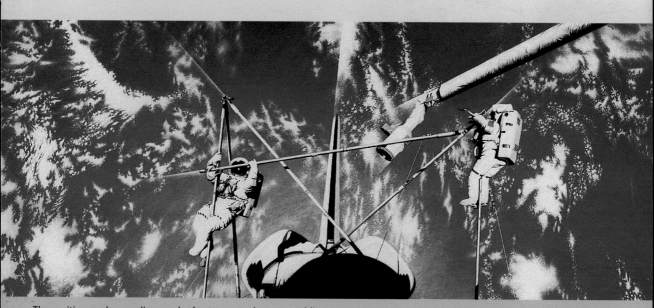

The exciting and rewarding work of astronauts, here assembling a space station, is the foundation of America's space program.

I N D E X